The Ultimate Guide to Money Spells

From the series:
The Ultimate Guide to Magick

Also by S. R. Gray:

Blank Book of Shadows

Coming Soon:

The Ultimate Guide to Love Spells
The Ultimate Guide to Protection Spells

Find me online:

Facebook: Lady Gray Witch
Instagram: @lady.gray.witch
Email: lady.gray.witch@gmail.com

Illustrations by S.R.Gray

Index

Introduction

What's up witches? Are you ready to make some money? I know I am! Life is quite the rollercoaster but while the ups and downs are inevitable, we can take back control of situations that seem hopeless with the power that resides within us. If you are wondering whether or not you have the power, trust me, you do. You are worthy because you exist and you are more powerful than you think.

Everything you've ever wanted is made up of energy that vibrates at a certain frequency. If you match that frequency it's only a matter of time before you attract it to you like a magnet. For humans, the strongest vibration is generated through emotion, which is why in spellwork it is extremely important to feel all the feelings associated with having it now.

For more than 10 years I've been studying how to play with this energy and it has changed my life in many ways. Money magick has gotten me out of desperate circumstances that seemed completely helpless. Everyone goes through rough patches in life where finances are tight, even when you're out there working your ass off. You know as well as I do that the one constant in life is bills, while the inflow of money is variable. Magick can be the ace up your sleeve that changes things for the better. My spellwork has manifested hard cash out of nowhere, and has helped me overcome financial legal matters.

All of the spells in this book are meant to be versatile and adaptable. If you have a particular deity that you prefer to work with for all of your spellwork then please feel free to incorporate them as needed. The same goes for other ritualistic practices such as casting a circle, calling upon the elements and blessing the space. The more personalized you make the spell, the more powerful it will be, so I encourage you to explore!

Spells 101

The basics

What is a spell?

By definition, a spell is a series of words or actions used to manifest magical change. It's basically a physical crystallization of an intention. We can use words, tools and actions to help us achieve a state of optimal vibrational synchronization. In layman terms, they can help us feel the feelings of already having the thing we want and therefore match that vibration and draw it to us. The amount of effort, detail and energy that you put into a spell represent your dedication to reaching your goal and will directly impact the outcome.

Why Cast?

Maybe your car broke down, or your credit card debt is piling up. Perhaps you're being chased down by student loans or your job isn't paying you enough to pay the rent AND get groceries. Maybe you just need some extra cash or maybe you desperately need to get out of a sticky situation. There are so many reasons to attract more money and almost all of them are valid. Some might say the only reason to avoid money spells might be when the intention is strictly greedy or when the spell will have a negative effect on other people. Money is not inherently evil but when the love for money infringes on love itself, it can create bad karma. I do believe that spells can work even when the intention is powered by greed, but these spells can have side effects and might come with some negative karma.

When to cast?

You can generally cast spells whenever you want but certain moon phases and planetary influences can add extra oomph to your magick. The timing of your spell will depend on the type of spell you're casting and your urgency. While most of us like to cast our spells after sunset, noon is known for being the ideal time for wealth and success spells. Having said that, casting any spell at midnight can be very powerful. Traditionally, money spells are best cast on a Thursday, the day associated with wealth, expansion and success. This doesn't mean that the spell won't be effective on any other day, it just means that the Thursday Jupiterian energies will add an extra layer of power to your workings. A great number of witches base their spell timing on the phases of the moon. A waxing moon symbolizes growth, so almost all wealth magick is performed during this period. Spells related to money may be performed during a waning moon when the focus is on decreasing or eliminating a financial obstacle such as debt or a legal matter. When in doubt, rest assured that any spell performed on the full moon will be boosted by the powerful full moon energies.

Money spell mechanics

Intention setting

The first part of a spell is figuring out the exact final outcome desired and summarizing it into an intention statement. This can be a written statement, a spoken declaration or a quiet awareness. Regardless of the form that it takes, the intention should be specific, personal and close to the heart. The most powerful spells are ones driven by powerful emotions, and that is why the matter at hand must be important to the caster.

A statement of intent should always be in the present tense, affirmative form. This means that the statement should not include negatives, and it should imply that you already have the desired outcome. A negative statement sounds something like, "I'm not broke anymore," while an affirmative version of that statement would sound like, "I'm becoming more financially stable." A common mistake is using future tense sentences like "I will receive more money," instead of the present tense version, which is so important for creating the vibration of having it now.

Stating that you want to receive "double your income" has more power than simply asking for "more money" because "double" has a very specific signature frequency, while "more" is infinitely broad and could range from a penny to infinity. It is easier to connect to something you desire when you can pinpoint it exactly. I like using "more than $x.xx" this way I'm setting a clearly defined baseline while leaving a little bit of room for error.

Planning and preparation

Determine the timing of the spell based on the type of intention and the level of urgency. Consider moon phases, day of the week, time of the day and planetary alignments.

You may choose to prepare yourself in advance for the spell as well. In the days leading up to the spell casting, some witches like to prepare by:
- Meditating
- Fasting
- Eating only certain foods
- Taking a cleansing bath
- Getting a blessing

- Saging their auras
- Spending time in nature

Find or write a spell. Memorize it if you can, or else write it on something you can keep handy during the casting. Gather all of the tools and supplies you will need for the spell and set everything up ahead of time (don't forget your lighter!). Once you start the spell you want everything to flow uninterrupted; nothing kills the mood like having to suddenly get up to go find something.

Opening

Most witches have some type of opening ritual that they perform before beginning spellwork. This is usually done to cleanse, protect and energize the space to facilitate the spell. This is recommended but not mandatory. Some of the most common techniques are:

- **Saging:** also known as "smudging" saging is the burning of dried sage leaves around the room and/or around the person in order to cleanse negative energy. Another benefit of burning sage is that it removes more than 90% of the bacteria in the air. You can use a ceremonial feather to direct the smoke or you can just let it burn. It also helps to say something out loud to communicate your intention, something like "With this sage I cleanse this space of any negative energies." In the absence of sage, you can use salt water in a spray bottle to achieve the same effect.
- **Casting a Circle:** This is the practice of drawing a circle around the magical work space (typically with salt) for protection, purification and energetic amplification. The circle acts as a portal to the spirit realm and works as a bubble in which creative energy is amplified. To begin casting a circle, purify your space using your preferred cleansing method. Delineate the physical perimeter of your circle using salt, rocks, rope, branches or any other material that feels right. The circle should be wide enough for you to lie down in it. Set up your work space including every item you will need during the ritual. Position Four Corner correspondences in each quarter if you chose to incorporate this practice. At this point you may choose to activate or bless the circle by walking around it clockwise (also known as deosil) while sprinkling salt (optional) and stating its purpose out loud. The number of times you walk around the circle can be modified. If you have a particular number that is meaningful to you, use that number. I find that often the higher the number, the higher the charge. If you're unsure of what to say you can research elaborate circle casting incantations or you can simply use "Three times I walk and three times I talk. The circle is cast, all evil is blocked." At this point you may begin your ritual, but if

you have to leave your circle unexpectedly, it is customary to cut an ethereal opening with your athame or wand and seal it back up. When you are done, you will close the circle by walking counterclockwise (also known as widdershins) and stating out loud that the circle is being released.

- **Calling the Four Corners:** This is a short opening ritual that involves calling upon the four directions of Earth and the corresponding elements that they represent. The purpose of this ritual is to ask for protection and assistance. To begin you will choose your quarter calls, which are statements directed at each of the corners with the intention of calling upon their power and activating them. There is a plethora of quarter calls available online and in books that you can use, or you can decide to write your own to make them more personal. You can address the quarters as "Guardians", "Watchtowers", "Elements" or "Spirits". The directions and the elements can also be used interchangeably: north/earth, east/air, south/fire and west/water. The call can be different for each quarter but they should all ask for some type of assistance, such as protection, blessing, amplification, grounding, and manifestation. It should be something along the lines of "Watchtowers of the East, I call upon you to…" You might also choose to include items that correspond to each element: Earth can be represented by soil, stones, wood or a green candle. Incense, feathers or a yellow candle can symbolize air. Fire is traditionally represented by a candle and the color red. Water, shells or a blue candle can be used to represent water. When you are ready to begin calling upon the four corners, you will start by facing north and stating your quarter call with confidence while lighting the corresponding candle, if you're using one, or pointing your wand or athame in that direction. Moving clockwise, face each direction and recite your calls. It is also common to release each quarter at the end of your spellwork by either extinguishing the candles (this time counterclockwise starting with the last one lit) or making a closing statement for each quarter. A closing statement should include gratitude for the assistance received and a mention that the energies of each corner are now released.
- **Evoking a deity:** This is the practice of inviting a deity into your sacred space, and is not to be confused with "invoking" which is the practice of inviting a deity to possess your body. It is not necessary to evoke a deity when performing spellwork, however many witches who have developed a relationship with a particular deity like to invite them to participate in their rituals for an added boost of power. Keep in mind these deities are not obligated to accept an invitation, but there are things that you can do to entice their participation.
  - Bring an offering into the circle or leave an offering at an appropriate location before the spell. Research your deity to find out the specific types of offerings they prefer.

- If applicable, draw the deity's sigil inside the circle either on the ground or on a piece of paper.
- Find a prayer that has been historically used to evoke the deity of interest. If you can't find one, feel free to write one of your own or simply call out the deity's name and ask them to join you.

You may decide to combine multiple opening rituals that resonate with you. If you feel unsure about any of them I recommend at least burning sage to begin with.

State of consciousness

The state of mind that is the most conducive to energy work and that allows you to become more receptive and creative is called the Alpha state. This state can be achieved when you slow your brain waves to about 8-12 Hz through meditation or hypnosis. It allows you to have access to your subconscious while still maintaining a certain level of consciousness. As you know, in order to attract and manifest something, you must first adjust your vibrations to match that frequency. Matching a frequency is done by experiencing the thoughts and emotions of already having it. The conscious mind can easily state an affirmation, but do you really FEEL it in your bones? After you've said you're affirmation and you go about your day, do you still feel that blissful feeling? Or does your mind have a tendency to go back to autopilot, where old belief systems hold the reigns? This is where the power of your subconscious comes into play. The subconscious mind learns through repetition and is responsible for holding belief systems that control the refrigerator hum of emotions that you experience throughout the day. This is why soaking an affirmation into your subconscious through meditation can be so powerful. At some point during your spell you should incorporate a meditation where you program the belief of having achieved the desired outcome into your subconscious.

Crystallization

In spellwork, crystallization is the transmutation of an intention into a physical object or action. In simple terms, it is a physical object or action that represents your intention. Some of the most common crystallizing actions include: verbally stating, writing, drawing, burning, folding, burying, shaking, tossing, stirring, knotting, dancing and walking. Some of the most common crystallizing objects include: candles, images, herbs, crystals, scents, natural objects, symbols, poppets and personal items. A crystallizing object or action should be something that you associate with your goal. You may choose to only use one, but generally speaking the more detail and effort you put into a spell the better the results.

Release

During the phases of meditation and crystallization, what you are doing is building up the energy of the spell. Traditionally, one final action is executed to officially release the built up energy into the Universe and set things in motion. Actions that could be considered release-actions include: burning, cutting, sealing, reciting a final incantation, burying or a symbolic gesture.

Take action

Once the spell is cast, everything is put away and you're carrying on with your day, there is one more thing you have to do to see results. You must take action, within reason, that facilitates the desired result. For example, if you are casting a spell to land a new job, you ought to start putting in applications and showing up to interviews. It's going to be pretty hard to get a new job if you're just glued to your couch all day. Identify things that you can do in your daily life that can help put you in a better position to receive your desired outcome.

Writing your own money spell

1) **Determine intention:** Figure out if your purpose is to draw money in or to eliminate a specific impediment. Determine the exact amount that you need and the timing of the manifestation. If you're removing a blockage, determine the root cause of the blockage. You can write out your intention in a single, present tense, positive statement. The statement should imply that you already have the desired result.

2) **Choose tools that correspond with that intention:** See page 17 for a complete list of tools. Choose the ones that resonate with you the most, but don't stress over obtaining ingredients that may take a long time and a hefty fee to obtain. While it is true that the more blood, sweat and tears you put into a spell the stronger the results, you shouldn't be discouraged from performing magic if you're a witch on a budget. The truth is you can use whatever ingredients you want because the most powerful and most important ingredient is your belief.

3) **Choose one or more actions:** Write, draw, burn, fold, bury, shake, hold, toss, fill, empty, stir, knot, or dance. These are some of the most common actions carried out during spells. Choose the ones that allow you to feel the power of manifestation. Actions that draw money energy towards you include folding a paper towards you and turning it clockwise, burning a green or gold candle, filling a jar with honey or Money Drawing Oil, stirring clockwise, tying a knot and burying something in your front lawn. Actions that banish energetic blockages are, tossing something over your shoulder, burying something in your backyard, graveyard or crossroads, turning something upside-down, burning a black candle and undoing a knot.

4) **Write an incantation (optional):** an incantation is a series of spoken words that have the power of realizing an intent. The key to writing a spell is to creatively state that the ingredients and actions in the spell are working to manifest the desired outcome. It doesn't have to rhyme and there's no minimum amount of words required. I personally find that rhyming can help me remember the spell and make it more powerful. You can research elaborate pre-made spells if you don't feel comfortable writing our own. I always recommend personalizing as much as you can, so if you can't find the perfect one online or in a book, modify an existing one or start from scratch (Disclaimer: don't do this if you're evoking a demon, stick to the script).

5) **Set up beforehand:** Find a quiet space where you know you won't be interrupted. While a beautiful mystical forest might be the romantically ideal location, city witches have to adapt and work with what they have. As long as you're in an environment where you can focus and execute the spell without major interruptions, you should be fine. Be aware of

things like smoke detectors, open windows, pets (your cat wants to participate), house alarms and anything that could cause an interruption. When setting up your space for the ritual, go over your entire spell plan and make sure you set up every tool needed in advance. It's good practice to make a checklist for elaborate spells. If you have multiple incantations, organize them by order of execution. Don't forget the lighter.

6) **Cast the spell in confidence:** Now that you've put all of this work into the prep and everything is set up, it's showtime. The smoother the execution is the stronger the spell will be because you'll be able to maintain sharp focus throughout the stages. It's a good idea to memorize your incantations but I recommend having the written incantation readily available in case you forget. I also recommend going through the order of things a few times in your head before performing elaborate spells. During your spellwork, speak with confidence and act with determination. If you feel like shouting, don't hold back. Take your time with the meditation and allow all of the feelings to fully develop unrestricted. Trust your instincts and if at any point you feel silly, know that that's normal and that your actions hold more power than a fleeting feeling of silliness.

Tools for the task

Herbs

Different plants contain different energies and some are known for vibrating at a frequency that draws in abundance. There are several ways to incorporate herbs into your spellwork. You can combine herbs in a small bag and carry it with you to attract good luck and success. This practice is called sachet magick. You can also use herbs in the form of incense, or you can burn them along with your written intention. It is common to dress candles with herbs that match the spell intention. It is also common to incorporate them in Money Drawing oils, and some witches like to place them in their bath water to help them soak up the corresponding vibrations. Don't be afraid to be creative and incorporate the herbs that resonate with you in a way that feels right for you. Some of the most commonly used abundance herbs include:

Mint: helps draw in money and peace of mind.

Basil: can help with business challenges, also attracts peace and happiness.

Cinnamon: considered by some to be the most powerful of money drawing herbs cinnamon brings luck in business, gambling and love.

Chamomile: can draw money and prosperity towards you.

Pine: attracts wealth and good luck.

Ginger: can be used to attract money and increase the speed of the manifestation. It also protects against negative energies.

Alfalfa: can help prevent poverty.

Pennyroyal: can help draw in customers and bring in more business and prosperity.

Irish moss: can attract money and good luck.

Allspice: known to bring money, luck and healing.

Thyme: powerful money attractor.

Cloves: brings winnings at games of chance. Also helps with love and protection.

Bay leaf: can help with promotions, new jobs, and just about anything when the intention is written directly on the leaf.

Frankincense: can bring successful outcomes for meetings and interviews.

Bergamot: can be rubbed on money to make it multiply and return to you.

Tonka bean: can draw financial abundance toward you when you carry it with you.

Poppy seeds: bring good fortune and abundance.

Almond: helps draw in money when carried on your person.

Nutmeg: can increase money and success.

Stones and Crystals

The energetic signature of stones and crystals has been recognized for centuries. They are known for balancing and directing energies, and they can provide a powerful boost when it comes to spellwork. Most of these can be found at gift shops, specialty stores and occult shops. Crystals can be used in the same way herbs are used, but keep in mind some of them can be damaged by water. It is good to wear them as jewelry and keep them on your body all the time. Since the number eight is associated with wealth, some witches like to collect eight crystals and use them together. You can place them in the southwest corner of your home to facilitate the flow of abundance. The most commonly used crystals are:

Iron pyrite: also known as Fool's Gold, this is one of the most popular crystals used to attract money. It helps overcome financial hardships through wisdom and perseverance. It also helps ignite thoughts of abundance and can boost vitality.

Citrine: also known as the Lucky Merchants stone, it has a light energy and is known for being one of the best crystals for wealth. It can increase the speed of manifestation and it is particularly advantageous to business owners. It helps you keep money in addition to attracting it.

Aventurine: is known for being the Stone of Opportunity and helps with new business ventures. It has an adventurous energy and it brings good luck with gambling. It helps you seize opportunities you may otherwise have missed.

Tiger's eye: will help you see things from different perspectives and find diverse pathways to success. Will also help you stay grounded and motivated in the face of challenge. Great stone for manifestation, especially when combined with other wealth stones.

Amazonite: can vanquish energy blockages and bring hope. It can reignite your passion for your work and boost your leadership skills. Brings success and abundance in business.

Malachite: has the power to remove negative energies. Can transform feelings of lack into motivation and empowerment. This stone is great for getting out of debt.

Green jade: can help you achieve your long term financial goals through hard work and consistency. It also helps remove self-imposed blockages and limitations. Great for business owners.

Amethyst: is known for clearing the mind and helping make better decisions. can be used for pretty much any spell.

Peridot: this stone has a light and positive energy that helps inspire feelings of worthiness and abundance while reducing self-limiting beliefs about money.

Clear Quartz: can be used for anything as it amplifies energy. Can be used on its own to amplify the energy of an intention or it can be combined with other crystals to amplify their energy.

Oils

Oils can be used to anoint candles and activate the object of the spell. The most commonly used oil for money spells is called Money Drawing Oil and it can be found online or at your local occult store. You can also make your own by following one of the many recipes available. Typically the potion is comprised of an oil base (olive, coconut etc.) infused with herbs that are known to attract money and abundance. Recipes may include: alfalfa, allspice, basil, chamomile, citrine, clove, bayberry, mint, cinnamon, irish moss, pine, citrine, aventurine and iron pyrite.

Easy Money Drawing Oil recipe: Fill a small bottle with olive oil and add basil, chamomile, cinnamon and iron pyrite (optional). If you want, you can charge the bottle with your intention or with moon light.

Incense

Scent has a way of changing your mood and creating an atmosphere. For centuries incense has been used to help manifest intention. Use scents to help you match abundance vibrations during meditations and rituals. Some of the ones most commonly used for wealth magick include:

Cinnamon: has a sweet fragrance that helps inspire feelings of abundance and worthiness.
Pine: has an uplifting, energizing scent that awakens intuition and inspires a positive work ethic.
Frankincense: can be used to attract power and wealth especially when combined with other prosperity scents.
Clove: helps reveal and overcome financial blockages including fears and self-limitations.
Citrus: has a revitalizing scent that helps energize you to accomplish your goals, and brings good fortune.
Jasmine: can help attract both money and love as it strengthens your power of attraction.
Patchouli: has an earthy scent that boosts your power of attraction for both money and seduction.
Vanilla: has that sweet, familiar scent that reminds you of home and comfort.
Saffron: helps inspire confidence in your creative abilities, and boosts your power of financial manifestation.
Honeysuckle: has a sweet scent known for drawing in wealth and luxury.
Cardamom: has a stress relieving scent that helps you feel grounded and optimistic.
Vetiver: is particularly good for ending vicious cycles and turning situations around for the best.

Candles

Burning candles is one of the oldest, most popular practices in witchcraft. The magick can lie in the color of the candle or in the flame itself depending on your intention. When it comes to color, **green** and **gold** are the best colors for money magick. **White** can always be used as a substitute, and you can also use **black** if your intention is to remove a blockage.

When choosing a candle, make sure that the size is suitable for the timing of the spellwork you have planned. Some spells require the candle to burn all the way down, in which case a smaller candle would be more efficient.

Don't recycle used candles for spellwork unless you are only using it for the flame. Many believe that candles absorb the energy from a spell and that if you try to use the same candle again for a different spell, that stored energy could interfere with your new intention. For the same reason, it is customary to save the remains of a burnt down spell candle and either store it or bury it somewhere meaningful.

Another common practice is to cleanse, dress and bless your candle before use.

- **Cleansing**: You can cleanse a candle by smudging it or passing it through incense smoke. Alternatively you could lightly spray it with salt water or bury it temporarily.
- **Dressing**: This is the practice of rubbing oils like Money Drawing Oil and prosperity herbs onto the candle. You may also choose to carve names, words and symbols that represent your intention.
- **Blessing**: You can bless the candle by saying a prayer over it or by simply holding it while visualizing your desired outcome. If you're using visualization, see the candle glowing with energy in your mind's eye.

Fire safety

Always use fire safety while doing spellwork, you'd be surprised how quickly a situation can get out of hand.

- Make sure candles are secure and stable.
- If you have pets, don't leave the candle unattended.
- Be aware of the candle's surroundings. Avoid any surface that has fabric or flammable materials hanging above it.
- Make sure the candle is placed on a surface that can safely collect dripping wax.

Make Your Spells Work

The Power of Belief

I couldn't write a book of spells without mentioning how important the power of belief is. The individual tools that we use don't hold any supernatural power of their own, but it is our belief and intention that breathes life into our spellwork. This is why it is important that you chose spells that you truly believe will work for you. If you are new to spellwork I recommend you start with smaller spells and gradually work your way up as you gain experience.

A word about gratitude

The majority of the spells in this book incorporate gratitude for a reason. Gratitude is the energetic fuel that brings us what we truly desire: more reasons to be grateful. All of the different objects, experiences and feelings that we desire all have one thing in common; once we finally get them, we feel grateful. The universal law dictates that like attracts like, therefore feeling grateful will inevitably attract more situations that will make us feel grateful. Abundance is a mindset driven by gratitude.

How to use these spells

The rest of this book is comprised of practical spells that you can either use as an example for inspiration or that you can follow directly to obtain results. These spells are organized based on purpose.

Make sure you read through the whole spell before you begin performing it. It is best to gather all items needed before hand to ensure smooth operation. I recommend opening and closing a circle around your workspace and saging/blessing as needed.

The spells can also be cast on behalf of someone else. Simply replace your name with theirs while following the instructions.

When it comes to deadlines, you can add a specific timing into your spell by simply adding it into the statement of intent. If you are working a petition spell, add the deadline to the petition. If you are using spoken statements, include the preferred timing. If you are working with visualizations, see the date in your mind's eye.

I wish you the best of luck on your creative journey, may you be blessed with abundance in every form!

Unexpected Income

There's nothing better than finding extra cash in your jeans or receiving an unexpected paycheck. With a little bit of magick, you can manifest these

scenarios at will!

Plant a seed

Purpose: To increase abundance gradually through multiple means, and to receive it in unexpected ways.

Moon Phase: waxing crescent or full moon.

Items needed:
A quiet space to meditate
Paper and pen
Fertile soil
Vase

1) Write the following sentence on a piece of paper with your own first and last name: "*Name's* divine seed of financial abundance".
2) Cut out the sentence so that all you have left is a long thin piece of paper. Roll it up into the shape of a pill.
3) Fill the vase half way with dirt using your hands, keeping in mind that the dirt represents the fertile soil of your subconscious.
4) Assume a meditative position, take deep breaths and begin to go deeper into a meditative state while holding the vase with both hands. Visualize yourself sinking into the ground of your own subconscious. Repeat the cycle of going deeper and deeper until you feel like you have significantly altered your state, and you have access to your subconscious. Now put down the vase, take the pill sized piece of paper and hold it in your hands while you visualize abundance. Visualize seeing a high balance in your bank account, your wallet being full of cash and expensive items displayed in your home.
5) Take the "seed" and plant it in the dirt knowing that you are planting it in your own subconscious.
6) Place the vase in your bedroom, and every day for seven days water the seed with both water and gratitude and then place a dollar in the vase.
7) At the end of the seven days, take the money out of the vase, put it in your wallet and spend it.
8) Transfer the dirt and "seed" into a mason jar and keep it on a shelf where the sunlight will shine on it. If the time comes that you absolutely have to get rid of it, try to bury it in a nice place.

Full moon coin

Purpose: to program a coin with wealth energy and charge it with full moon energy.

Moon phase: full moon.

Items needed:
Space where the moon is visible
Cauldron or bucket
$1 coin or gold coin

1) Fill the cauldron with water and place it directly in the moonlight for an hour or longer allowing it to charge.
2) Sit in front of the cauldron, place the palms of your hands on the surface of the water and meditate on the feeling of abundance. Visualize having more money and being able to spend it.
3) Drop the coin into the water, place your hands back onto the surface and recite the following words;
    a) "Moon water bless this coin of success.
       Wherever I go, my money will grow."
4) Take the index finger of your dominant hand and draw three circles in the water clockwise and say "So mote it be."
5) Take the coin out and keep it in your wallet or somewhere close. Pour the water at the base of the tree while thanking it for allowing you to charge your coin.

Enchanted wallet

Purpose: to enchant your wallet so that it attracts more cash to it.

Moon phase: waxing gibbous or full moon.

Items needed:
Wallet (optional: green or gold)
Small piece of iron pyrite
Bills
Coins
Bay leaf
Mint

1) Take out all of the contents of your wallet and lay them out on a table.
2) Throw away or store what you don't need to carry in your wallet.
3) Rub mint leaves in your hands while saying "Amplify and intensify." The more repetitions, the better.
4) Take all of the coins in the palms or your hands and recite the following words:
   a) "Thank you for being in my wallet, call your brothers and sisters to join you. This is your new home."
5) Take each card, one at a time, and rub your fingers on them while saying:
   a) "Thank you for being in my wallet. Always paid and ready to pay."
6) Take each paper bill starting with the lowest one and repeat the words cited in step 4.
7) Write the words "money magnet" on the bay leaf, thank it for attracting more money and put it in one of the pockets of your wallet.
8) Once everything is back in the wallet, hold it and visualize a green light emanating from it, a light that indicates that the wallet is actively pulling more money towards it like a magnet.

Money bowl

Purpose: to create a beacon that attracts more money into your home.

Moon phase: waxing moon or full moon.

Items needed:
Gold or green glitter (optional)
Money Drawing Oil (optional)
Chamomile flowers
Iron pyrite
Small bowl
Basil leaves
Pine needles
Mint leaves
Coins
Jewelry

1) Place a few coins in the bowl one at a time saying the following words for each coin:
   a) "Thank you for coming into my hands, call your brothers and sisters to join us."
2) Place the iron pyrite and the jewelry into the bowl while saying:
   a) "These are the riches that multiply."
3) Sprinkle each herb into the bowl one at a time while you recite the following words:
   a) "Sprinkling *herb name* to amplify and intensify."
4) Optional: add Money Drawing Oil and glitter on top.
5) Every day for seven days add one coin to the bowl while reciting the coin statement from step 1. At the end of the week put the coins in your wallet and spend them. Repeat the cycle seven times.

Money tree

Purpose: to gradually increase income by expected and unexpected means.

Moon phase: waxing gibbous or full moon.

Items needed:
Potted mint plant
Iron pyrite
Watering can

1) Dig a small hole in the dirt around the mint plant and bury the piece of iron pyrite.
2) Put water in the watering can and hold it in your hands while you recite the following words:
   a) "I bless this water with my heart,
      every atom and every part.
      grow this plant and grow my treasure,
      bring abundance beyond measure."
3) Keep this enchanted water on the windowsill and use it to water your mint plant only. Say the incantation from step 2 once or twice a week to keep it charged.

Pine Cone

Purpose: to plant the seed to attract more cash from unknown sources.

Moon phase: waxing crescent or full moon.

Items needed:
Lined paper and pen
Cauldron or pot
Pine cone
Money oil
Cinnamon

1) After setting up your sacred space, take a lined piece of paper and write out everything you would do if you had a lot more money. Fill the entire page, it's ok if you have to repeat. Write everything in the present tense and start off with "I am so grateful for all the extra money I have, now I can buy/do/go…"
2) Fold the paper three times toward yourself.
3) Using fire safety, burn the paper and collect the ashes. Make sure every part is fully burned.
4) Dress the pine cone with Money Drawing Oil using either a brush or your fingers.
5) Roll the pine cone in the ashes trying to collect as much of the ashes onto the pine cone as you can.
6) Bury the pine cone, along with the rest of the ashes, in your front yard. If you don't have any type of yard nearby, you can bury it in a vase filled with dirt. You can also put fake or real flowers in the vase as a disguise.

Abundance bath

Purpose: to bathe yourself in abundance energy and carry it with you throughout the day.

Moon phase: every quarter moon starting the night of the new moon leading up to the full moon.

Items needed:
Candles and incense (optional)
Chamomile
Lemongrass
Bath tub
Honey
Citrine
Mint

1) Draw a warm bath, light candles and incense.
2) Place the Citrine in the water.
3) One by one, sprinkle each herb generously over the bath water while reciting the following words:
   a) "I bathe in *herb name* body and soul.
      Wealth vibrations fill this bowl."
4) In your mind's eye, see the bath emanating a golden energy that vibrates at the frequency of wealth and prosperity.
5) Drizzle a circle of honey onto the surface of the warm water while reciting the following incantation:
   a) "Honey is gold, sweet and thick.
      Honey will make this energy stick."
6) Slowly get into the bathtub and focus on the feeling of the warm water/wealth energy covering your body. Enjoy your bath!
7) When you feel ready to be done, drain the bath water, collect the herb residue and dispose of it in nature.
8) Keep the citrine in your wallet, purse or pocket.

Note: If you don't have a bath tub, put the herbs and honey in a cloth pouch and rub it gently against your skin in the shower.

Knots

Purpose: to use knots to aid your creative process of attracting more money.

Moon phase: first quarter or full moon. Waxing phases will do the trick as well.

Items needed:
12-15 inch green string
10 Mint leaves

1) Lay out the string and 10 mint leaves on your workspace.
2) Tie a leaf into a knot in the string close to one end. While you are tying the knot recite the following incantation:
   a) "The first knot is tied, the energy applied. My money is increasing"
3) Tie the next leaf about an inch away from the last one, and continue in this pattern while reciting one incantation per knot:
   a) "The second knot is tied, the energy applied. I have more money than expected."
   b) "The third knot is tied, the energy applied. My wallet is full of cash."
   c) "The fourth knot is tied, the energy applied. I have money in the bank."
   d) "The fifth knot is tied, the energy applied. I can buy whatever I want."
   e) "The sixth knot is tied, the energy applied. My savings are growing."
   f) "The seventh knot is tied, the energy applied. All my bills are paid."
   g) "The eighth knot is tied, the energy applied. Money comes easily."
   h) "The ninth knot is tied, the energy applied. Money comes frequently."
   i) "The tenth knot is tied, the energy applied. I am filled with gratitude."
4) Hang the string on the wall above your bed and repeat the incantations while touching each mint leaf every night before bed.

Specific amount

Knowing the exact amount of money that you need can be a huge advantage when i
t comes to spell casting. The digits carry a specific frequency that is readily available for

you to pinpoint and draw towards you.

Bay leaf

Purpose: to attract a specific amount of money from an unspecified source.

Moon phase: waxing and full moon preferred.

Items needed:
Cauldron or pot
Pen and paper
Bay leaf

1) Write the amount of money you need on a bay leaf. If the number is greater than 100, break it down to increments of 100 per bay leaf. For example, if the amount you needed was $575.00 you would have 5 bay leaves with $100 written on them and one with $75.
2) Using fire safety, burn the bay leaves while reciting the following words:
    a) "Bay leaf burn, bay leaf rise,
       Bring X.XX before my eyes.
       Bring it fast and bring it soon.
       By my will and by the moon."
3) Bury the ashes in your front lawn while thanking them for bringing you the amount you needed.

Paper wallet

Purpose: to manifest an exact amount of money by unspecified means.

Moon phase: first quarter and full moon.

Items needed:
Green or gold glitter
Paper and pen
Green candle
Cinnamon
Bay leaf

1) On a piece of paper about the size of a credit card, write "*Name's* wallet" filling in your full name.
2) Keep this paper in your wallet for a week or longer in order to create an energetic link between the two.
3) Prepare your space and light the candle.
4) Write on the bay leaf the exact amount of money you want to manifest.
5) Using fire safety, burn the bay leaf using the flame of the candle and collect the ashes.
6) Take the paper out of your wallet and place it on a disposable surface such as a paper plate.
7) Sprinkle the ashes, cinnamon and glitter onto the paper.
8) Drip candle wax onto the paper while reciting the following incantation:
   a) "Green wax drip and seal the deal
      Make $x.xx become real."
9) Store the paper on a shelf near your front door.

You've got mail

Purpose: to mail an enchanted envelope to yourself in order to disperse the energy of the spell into the system and bring it back to you.

Moon phase: first quarter and full moon.

Items needed:
Blank check (optional)
Paper and pen
Basil leaves
Mint leaves
Envelope
Stamp

1) Either print out a faux blank check or do your best to draw a replica on a piece of paper.
2) On the top left corner, replace the issuing company name with the words "New Source". If you already know of a specific source that could generate the amount of money that you need, use the name of that source instead.
3) Fill out the check and write the exact amount of money that you want to attract.
4) Put the check in the middle of your work space and then place one basil leaf and one mint leaf on each corner of the paper moving clockwise.
5) Rub your hands together and begin to enter a meditative state.
6) Hover your hands above the check once you feel like they are charged with energy. Begin to visualize everything you will do once you receive the money, and feel the feelings of gratitude as deeply as you can.
7) Push this energy from your hands into the check. Visualize the check glowing with yellow and green light.
8) When it feels charged, collect the check and leafs and place them in the envelope.
9) Seal the envelope while reciting:
    a) "Here and now I seal the deal,
        Manifesting this gratitude I feel."
10) Mail the envelope to yourself right away.
11) When you receive the envelope, open it as if you weren't expecting it. When you see the check, rejoice and give thanks for receiving the money.
12) Put the check in your wallet and keep the leafs by your bedside.

Banishing debt

If you feel like you're drowning in debt or you've got bills weighing on your shoulders, magick can help you regain confidence in your creative abilities, even when the situation seems helpless.

Extension needed

Purpose: to influence the payee of your bill to give you an extension. This works best when the payee knows you personally, like a landlord.

Moon phase: any phase will do but waxing gibbous and full moon are best.

Items needed:
Company logo
Licorice root
Chamomile
Tinfoil
Jar

1) Cut out the company logo or draw a replica. If there is no logo, write the name of the payee on a small piece of paper.
2) Wrap the paper, licorice and chamomile in a piece of tinfoil. If you can obtain an image of the payee, or something that the payee has touched, add that as well.
3) Wrap more tinfoil around the bundle shaping it into a small poppet.
4) Hold the poppet in your hands and focus on the vibration of the payee creating an energetic link between the two. Repeatedly say the payee's name out loud while looking directly at it until you feel like it's charged.
5) Place the poppet in the jar and begin to pour honey all over it while reciting the following incantation:
   a) "*Payee name*, I have control
      Over your mind and over your soul.
      This is my command to you:
      Kindly change when the payment's due."
6) Completely cover the poppet in honey, seal the jar and store it in your attic. If you don't have an attic, store it on the highest shelf you have.

Bill be gone

Purpose: to be able to pay off a bill or have it waived.

Moon phase: a waning moon will do the trick, but a new moon will have the strongest results.

Items needed:
Olive oil or substitute oil
Mint or bay leaves
Invoice or bill
Black pepper
Envelope

1) Put a small amount of oil in a small dish and mix it with black pepper and crushed leaves.
2) Locate these three things on your bill:
    a) The name/logo of the company
    b) The amount owed
    c) The due date
3) Dip your thumb in the oil just enough to get a finger print's worth of oil.
4) Recite the following words:
    a) "Bill be gone, bill be gone!
       It's paid, it's paid, it's paid.
       No more bill, no more bill.
       It's paid just like I prayed."
5) When you're saying "it's paid" three times in a row put a thumb print on each of the three items listed in step 2.
6) Fold the bill to fit into an envelope on the back of which you will write "PAID" .
7) Store the envelope face up so that you see the word "PAID" every time you look at it.

Sticky business

Purpose: to eliminate a bill by rendering it void. This spell is meant to make the bill magically disappear due to error rather than to obtain money to pay it off.

Moon phase: new moon.

Items needed:
Blackstrap molasses
1 Cupcake liner
Licorice candy
Black candle
Black marker
Bill or invoice
Black string

1) Cut the licorice into small pieces and mix them into 1 cup of molasses. Heat the mixture for 30 seconds (don't let it boil).
2) Light the black candle.
3) Take the bill (or a copy of it) and write the words "void" and "waived" in big letters all over the bill, especially where the total amount is listed.
4) Fold the paper once away from you and then drip wax from the black candle in between the two sides so that they stick together.
5) Turn the paper counterclockwise and fold it away from you again, adding more wax to make it stick.
6) Repeat this step three more times until it is small enough to fit into a cupcake liner.
7) Wrap it in black string and tie a knot so that it stays folded.
8) Place it in the cupcake liner and then pour the mixture from step 1 on top while repeating the following incantation:
    a) "Molasses dark as night,
       Take this bill out of sight.
       Take this bill out of mind,
       Somewhere no one can find."
9) Bury the cupcake liner in a graveyard as deep as you can. As you cover it with dirt, visualize being told you don't have to pay the bill due to some random error. When you

walk out of the graveyard, forget all about the bill and the spell, and actively keep your mind off of the subject.

Banishing Spiral

Purpose: to banish any form of debt from credit card debt to loans.

Moon phase: a waning moon will do the trick, but a new moon will have the strongest results.

Items needed:
Black pen or marker
Black pepper
Paper

1) Cut out a paper square about the size of your hand.
2) Rub black pepper on both sides of the paper.
3) Write out the words "I currently owe $" including the total amount that you owe.
4) Take a moment to neutralize any feelings associated with that.
5) Turn the paper counterclockwise a quarter of the way and then write over the previous sentence "I currently owe $" including **half** of the total amount that you owe. At this point the two sentences should cross at a perpendicular angle.
6) Take a moment to think about what it will feel like to have half of all your debt paid off. Visualize yourself and others appreciating your progress.
7) Turn the page counterclockwise again and write the words "I currently owe $0.00" on top of the previous words.
8) Take a moment to meditate intensely on the feeling of having paid off all of your debt. Imagine telling friends and family and seeing the balance in your account. Think about all the ways in which your life is improved by paying off your debt.
9) Turn the paper counterclockwise again and write the word "PAID" on top of the previous words.
10) Turn the paper counterclockwise one last time and and draw a spiral counterclockwise starting from the edges of the paper and moving inwards. When you reach the center lift the pen straight up towards the sky to release the energy into the Universe.
11) Place the paper under your pillow and sleep on it every night until your debt is gone.

Sour Debt

Purpose: to eliminate debt gradually in the time that is takes for a lemon to decompose.

Moon phase: a waning moon will do the trick, but a new moon will have the strongest results.

Items needed:
Plastic wrap or tin foil
Paper and pen
Lemon
Pepper
Salt

1) On a small piece of paper, write the name of the company you are in debt with, and the total amount owed.
2) Cut the lemon in half and carve out a little bit from the middle of each half.
3) Mix salt and pepper in a small bowl. Draw clockwise circles in the mixture with your index finger while reciting the following words three times.
    a) "White salt pepper black, banish debt and banish lack."
4) Sprinkle the mixture on the inside of the lemon halves while saying:
    a) "Sour lemon eat away, the debt that I'm supposed to pay."
5) Insert the small piece of paper in one half of the lemon, join the two halves together and wrap it up so it won't fall apart.
6) Bury the lemon in a graveyard if you can. If you can't, find an adequate location somewhere relatively far from your home. Unwrap the lemon before you bury it and while you are doing so, thank it repeatedly for fading away your debt.

Getting paid

If you are willing to put in work, abundance is right around the corner for you, especially when you use magick to attract a job that suits you, and that pays enough to keep you satisfied.

Witch be hired

Purpose: to influence a specific company to hire you.

Moon phase: any phase will do but a waxing moon or a full moon are best.

Items needed:
Printed copy of a blank check
Logo of the company
Paper and pen
Envelope
Cash

1) Cut out the logo of the company you want to work for and glue/tape it to the blank check where the company name belongs. If you can't print, draw out the check and logo as best as you can.
2) Write your name in the recipient section and the amount you think the job will pay you regularly.
3) Put $10 or $20 cash in an envelope with the check and go out and spend it in small amounts. Keep the check in front of the cash so that you see it when you open the envelope.
4) Every time you take money out of the envelope, tell someone you don't know (like the cashier) that you got a new job.
5) Do this for a week and then burn the check and bury the ashes in your front lawn or somewhere meaningful.

Job Finder

Purpose: to get hired promptly by an employer in a certain geographical location. This spell is meant to be used before you start interviewing.

Moon phase: first quarter or full moon.

Items needed:
Tape, string or rubber band
Fresh basil leaves
Candle or lighter
Pen or marker
Paper map
Tiger's eye
Honey

1) On the map, draw a circle that encompasses the area of town you'd like to work in. This doesn't have to be a perfect circle
2) Drizzle honey all over the inside of the circled area. The honey will act as physical and ethereal glue.
3) Stick basil leaves on the honey inside the circled area and press them down with the palms of your hands. The fresh basil leaves represent fresh opportunities for you to bring in prosperity.
4) Place the tiger's eye, representing you in the center of the circle
5) Carefully, warm the circle by passing the paper over the flame. Keep it moving so that it doesn't actually burn through the paper. Do this slowly so that the Tiger's eye stays balanced.
6) While you're doing this, recite the following incantation:
    a) "Sacred fire of transformation,
       Bring me employment in this location.
       As the heat rises through the honey,
       So does opportunity for money."
7) Let the paper cool off while you meditate with the Tiger's Eye in your hand and visualize yourself having a job in the selected area. Imagine yourself being at your new job and feeling grateful for the success of your spell.

8) Carefully roll up the paper trying to keep the basil leaves within the circle, and seal it with tape, rubber band or string.
9) Bury the rolled up paper somewhere within the area of town that you circled on the map.
10) Keep the Tiger's Eye with you all the time, especially when filling in applications and interviewing.

NOTE: You can turn this into candle magick by using a gold, green or white candle and dressing it in one of the ways described in the Candle Magick chapter on page 21.

Interview

Purpose: to use a magick pouch to influence interviewers to choose you for the job.

Moon phase: any phase will do but waxing gibbous is best.

Items needed:
Fabric pouch
Paper and pen
Lavender
Mint
Sage
Dill
Basil

1) Cut out a medium sized circle of paper and write the following words repeatedly in a spiral starting from the edges moving to the center:
    a) "I was chosen for the job! I got the job!"
2) Fold the paper so that the writing is on the outside and place it in the pouch.
3) Visualize a green light projecting out of the pouch. Place the herbs in the pouch one by one while visualizing the light growing each time you add an herb.
4) Keep it in your purse, backpack or pocket and take it with you to your interview.

ChapStick Glamour

Purpose: to enchant your chapstick to enable you to give all of the right answers during your interview making you appear to be the most fit candidate for the job.

Moon phase: Any phase will do but waxing crescent is best.

Items needed:
Clear quartz
Chapstick
Lavender
Small bag
Sage

1) Smudge your chapstick before you begin.
2) Get into a meditative state and focus on the upcoming interview. See yourself answering questions eloquently, without hesitation. Imagine your interviewer looking impressed with what you are saying. Finally, visualize being told that you got the job.
3) Hold the chapstick and clear quartz in your hands while you push the energy of your visualization into the chapstick.
4) Recite the following incantation:
   a) "Let this tool hold this power,
   Every day and every hour,
   When I wear it I will know
   What to say to make me glow."
5) Immediately place the chapstick in a small bag with the quartz and the herbs.
6) Carry it with you to the interview and put the chapstick on right before you enter the building.

Business beehive

Purpose: to draw more customers to your business and to make it as busy as a beehive:

Moon phase: first quarter, waxing gibbous or full moon.

Items needed:
Honeysuckle candle
Honeycomb slice
Business card
Clear quartz
Honey
Jar

1) After setting up your ritual space and entering a meditative state, light the candle and hold the honeycomb slice while you think about what it looked like when it was part of a busy beehive. Visualize the scene in detail, and hear the buzzing sounds in your mind.

2) Hold this image and sound in your mind as you pick up your business card and begin to imagine the bees transforming into people as the beehive transforms into your business. See your shop filled with people, and imagine that the buzzing sound is coming from all of the customers.

3) Place the business card on the honeycomb and drip wax from the honeysuckle candle onto the edges of the card while reciting the following incantation:
   a) "Busy bee, busy me.
      Wax, merge this energy.
      Draw them in like bees to honey.
      Buzz into my store with money."

4) Place the honeycomb, business card and clear quartz into the jar and fill it to the top with honey. Keep the jar in your shop to act as a beacon to customers.

Getting approved

Waiting to hear if your loan has been approved can be quite nerve wracking...

unless you've cast a nifty little spell to sweeten up your odds!

Approval powder

Purpose: to create a powder that will increase your chances of being approved. This spell is meant to be worked before the application process begins.

Moon phase: waxing crescent or full moon.

Items needed:
Cinnamon powder
Mortar and pestle
Lemon grass
Chamomile
Iron pyrite
Citrine
Basil
Mint

1) Make sure all the herbs are dried.
2) Grind the herbs into a powder and mix them in a jar with the cinnamon.
3) Add the iron pyrite and citrine to the jar.
4) Hold the jar in your hands while you meditate on the feeling of having your loan approved. Visualize yourself thanking the loan agent repeatedly.
5) Repeat step 4 every day for as many days as you can leading up to the day you fill out the application. Visualize a green light emanating from the jar.
6) Before filling out the application, sprinkle or brush some of the Approval Powder on the application forms. If you're using a computer you can sprinkle or brush some onto the keyboard and mouse. If you're applying in an office and you don't want to spook people out, carry the mixture with you and get some on your hands before starting.

Agent Sweetener

Purpose: to influence your loan agent to feel an urge to push for your loan to be approved.

Moon phase: new moon or full moon. Waxing gibbous could also do the trick.

Items needed:
Name of your agent
Pen and paper
Licorice
Bay leaf
Honey
Jar

1) After setting up your space, write down the name of your agent on a small piece of paper. If you have their business card, you can use that instead.
2) Hold the piece of paper in your hand and think of their image. Visualize yourself thanking them for helping you get the loan.
3) Place the paper in a jar.
4) On the bay leaf, write the sentence:
   a) "Thank you for getting my loan approved."
5) Place the bay leaf in the jar.
6) Add licorice to the jar (this adds the power to influence).
7) Pour honey into the jar filling it enough to completely cover the contents. The more the better. While you're pouring, recite the following incantation.
   a) "Honey makes you sweet and honey makes you kind.
      Keep me in your heart and keep me in your mind mind.
      Do everything you can to get me this loan.
      Pull all the strings of the unknown."
8) Close the lid and seal it with candle wax (optional).
9) Hold the jar in your hands once a day until you hear the results. While holding it visualize yourself thanking the agent for all their help, and intensify your feelings of gratitude and relief from bing approved.

Credit score glamour

Purpose: to enchant your credit score to rise to the required score or more.

Moon phase: waxing gibbous or full moon.

Items needed:
2 printed copies of your credit score
Mint or basil leaves
Lighter or candle
Cauldron or pot
Pen or marker
Incense cone
White-out

1) On one of the copies of your credit score, white out the score numbers and replace them with the desired score. If they were originally written in color, use the same color ink or marker. The goal is for it to look as close to the original as possible.
2) Lay the two copies side by side.
3) Light the incense cone and place it in the cauldron/pot.
4) Using fire safety, burn the copy of your original credit score while simultaneously holding it above the incense smoke and reciting the following incantation:
   a) "Let this score be no more."
5) Wave the second "manifestation" copy above the incense smoke and recite:
   a) "Let this score replace what was once in place."
6) Rub the herbs onto the manifestation copy while visualizing everything that you are able to do with a higher credit score.
7) Tape or hang the manifestation copy on the wall above your bed.

Gambling/lottery

Is gambling really a gamble when the odds are on your side? Use magick to steer the

wheel of fortune. It will be our little secret.

Coin toss

Purpose: to use coin divination to determine lucky numbers.

Moon phase: new moon, waxing crescent or full moon.

Items needed:
Paper and pen
Chamomile
Red wine
7 coins
Chalice
Quartz

1) Write the numbers 1-9 on a piece of paper in large characters. Draw a circle around each number.
2) Fill a ritual cup with red wine, and place the quartz and the coins in the cup.
3) Hold the chamomile in your hands while you meditate on the feeling of winning. Thank the chamomile for blessing you with abundance.
4) Sprinkle chamomile in the wine while reciting the following incantation:
   a) "Chamomile flower, bless me with sight.
      Show me the winning numbers tonight."
5) Put your hand in the cup, shuffle around the coins and, when you feel ready, take one coin out of the cup.
6) Flip this coin above the paper 9 times. The first 6 numbers that the coin lands on are lucky numbers that can be combined with the remaining 3 to form double digit lucky numbers.
7) If you are having doubts about a number combination flip the same coin "heads/tails" style to clarify.
8) Write these numbers down and play them as soon as possible.

Aventurine meditation

Purpose: to retrieve lucky numbers from your Higher Self through meditation.

Moon phase: new moon, waxing crescent or full moon.

Items needed:
Quiet space
Aventurine
Incense

1) Prepare your quiet space for meditation and light incense.
2) Lie on your back in a comfortable position and place the aventurine on your forehead so that it lines up with your third eye.
3) Use breathing techniques to enter a meditative state and visualize your energy being cleansed.
4) Visualize yourself in a room that represents your subconscious. See the details of your subconscious room, and then turn your focus to a door. Imagine the details of this door, knowing that it is a door that leads to "the outside."
5) When you're ready, see yourself opening the door to a small open field in the middle of a forest. Walk across the open field and into the forest.
6) Search for an Abundance Tree. It will be a very large beautiful tree that is glowing with green energy. When you find it, it will have a predetermined number of medium stones laid out in a line at the base of it (depending on how many lucky numbers you need).
7) Ask the Abundance Tree to show you the lucky numbers for the specific game you are playing.
8) Turn the stones over quickly to reveal the lucky numbers and take note of them.
9) Thank the Abundance Tree and walk out of the forest, through the field and back into your subconscious room.
10) When you come out of meditation write down the numbers right away, and go play them!

Note: If you are having trouble revealing the numbers, you may be experiencing some doubt blockages. Don't get frustrated as things like this take time. Try again at a different time, spend more time going deeper into the meditation and cleansing your energy. Let go of all emotions and feelings of doubt.

Channeled choice

Purpose: to cast a spell on your hand to help you choose a winning scratch ticket.

Moon phase: waxing crescent or full moon.

Items needed:
Money drawing oil
Quiet space
Aventurine

1) The night before you purchase a scratch ticket, look up the process for claiming a winning ticket. Either look it up online or buy a scratch ticket just to read the back.
2) After setting up your space rub money drawing oil all over your dominant hand while visualizing yourself claiming the win, and thank the specific scratch ticket company for giving you money.
3) Wash your hands and return to meditation. This time hold the aventurine piece as you visualize telling all your friends and family that you won. Thank the aventurine for guiding you to pick the right ticket.
4) When you go to bed, hold on to the aventurine as you fall asleep while you visualize the desired outcome.
5) Before you leave the house in the morning rub money drawing oil on your dominant hand as described in step 2.
6) Wash your hands and carry the aventurine with you to the store.
7) When it's time to choose a ticket, hold the aventurine in your non dominant hand while you pick a ticket. Trust your inner voice and select swiftly without hesitation.

Jar Power

Purpose: to increase the chances of winning with a ticket for a lottery that hasn't been drawn yet.

Moon phase: any phase will do, full moon is best.

Items needed:
Lottery ticket
Aventurine
Bag of salt
Iron pyrite
Peridot
Mirror
Jar

1) Hold the stones in one hand and the lottery ticket in the other and read the back of the ticket where it explains what to do when you win. Read the instructions carefully and visualize yourself carrying out each step. Visualize the energy of the feeling of winning traveling from your head, down the arm and into the stones.
2) Place the stones in the jar and visualize the jar emanating a yellow light.
3) Roll up the lottery ticket carefully and place it in the jar.
4) Fill the jar with salt, leave it open and store it on a windowsill or somewhere where the light of the sun will shine on it.
5) Every day leading up to the draw, hold the jar in your hand and visualize yourself carrying out the steps to claim your prize. Feel gratitude for your newfound abundance.

Candle magick

Candle magick is one of the oldest and most popular forms of magick. It combines the element of fire with the specific frequency of colors. This makes candle magick an extremely powerful tool that you can use to draw in money. Be sure to read page 21 for details about how to select and use your candles.

Symbol candle

Purpose: to attract more money by unspecified means.

Moon phase: first quarter and full moon are best, but a waxing moon will do the trick.

Items needed:
Paper and green pen
Dried crushed basil
Money drawing oil
Green candle
Carving tool

1) Write your intentions on a piece of paper. Describe the final outcome you desire. Include details about how you will feel and act once you receive the extra money. Write it all in the present tense.
2) Look at what you have written and create a symbol that represents your desired outcome. It could be a symbol you have already seen before (like the dollar sign), it could be something you make up out of thin air, or it could be an actual sigil.
3) Cut out a small piece of paper about the size of a credit card and draw the symbol in green ink.
4) Writing over the symbol, fill the paper with the sentence "Thank you for this money" from top to bottom.
5) Carve the symbol that you came up with on the candle.
6) Dress the candle with oil and herbs while blessing it with your intention.
7) Place the candle directly on top of the small paper so that the candle wax will drip onto it.
8) Light the candle and recite the following incantation when the first drop of wax begins to fall:
    a) "Green onto green onto forces unseen,
       Bring me more riches than I can dream."
9) Let the candle burn until it is gone. Snuff it if you have to leave. When it's completely burnt out store it on a shelf.

Cinnamon Candle

Purpose: to attract more money by unspecified means.

Moon phase: first quarter and full moon are best, but a waxing moon will do the trick.

Items needed:
Coconut/olive oil
Paper and pen
Green candle
Cinnamon

1) Write a paragraph to describe how grateful you are for the money you have received up until now, and another paragraph to describe how grateful you will be upon receiving more money
2) Dress the candle with coconut or olive oil and sprinkle cinnamon while blessing the candle with thoughts and feelings of abundance.
3) Light the candle and burn the paper (using fire safety) while reciting the following incantation:
   a) "Sacred fire burn my words,
      Carry them far and fast.
      Bring to me this energy,
      Of abundance here at last."
4) Save the ashes and bury them in your front lawn or the closest thing you can find to a front lawn. Alternatively, if you live in the city, you can keep it by your windowsill or your front door.
5) Let the candle burn until it is gone. Snuff it if you have to leave. When it's completely burnt out, either bury it in your front yard or store it somewhere meaningful. Do not throw it into the trash or melt it into another candle as it still contains the energy of this spell.

Ashy business

Purpose: to attract abundance and situations/circumstances that make you feel wealthy.

Moon phase: first quarter and full moon are best, but a waxing moon will do the trick.

Items needed:
Paper and pen
Green candle
Sharp tool

1) Take a piece of lined paper and write each of the following sentences over and over until you reach the last line:
    a) "I am wealthy"
    b) "I have a lot of money"
    c) "I am grateful for all this cash"
2) Use a sharp tool to carve out your full name and date of birth on the candle starting from the top down.
3) Using fire safety, burn the paper with a lighter and collect the ashes.
4) Rub the ashes on the green candle from the top down while visualizing your hands holding lots of cash.
5) Place the remaining ashes at the base of the candle. Burn the candle until it is gone. Snuff it if you have to leave and bury or store the candle remains.

Abundance Jar

Purpose: to bring abundance in the form of cash from any source.

Moon Phase: first quarter or full moon.

Items needed:
Green or gold candle
Paper and pen
Gold glitter
Mint leaves
Iron Pyrite
Small jar

1) Write your full name on a small piece of paper. Optionally, you can mark it with your DNA (saliva, blood et.)
2) Write a paragraph (in the present tense) about all the things you intend to do with the extra cash you will receive and, at the end of the paragraph, write "Thank you."
3) Roll up the pieces of paper and place them in the jar.
4) Place mint leaves, iron pyrite and gold glitter in the jar on top of the papers. Put the lid on the jar.
5) Glue the candle to the lid of the jar.
6) Light the candle and make sure it drips wax onto the lid in order to seal the jar. As you're doing this recite the following incantation:
   a) "With this wax I seal the deal.
      As within so without.
      This abundance becomes real,
      Cash will come without a doubt."
7) Let the candle burn until it is gone. Snuff it if you have to leave and keep it by a window or your bedside.

Debt banishing candle

Purpose: to banish debt from one specific credit card company.

Moon phase: new moon is best, but a waning moon will work.

Items needed:
Paper and pen (or credit card if you're done using it)
Black pepper
Black candle
Tin foil

1) Take a small piece of tin foil about the size of your hand and place the credit card on top of it. If you are still actively using this card, cut out a piece of paper in the exact shape of the credit card and then copy the words, numbers and symbols of the credit card onto the front and back of the paper. Use this replica on the tinfoil instead of your actual card.
2) Take the black candle and dress it with black pepper. While you're dressing the candle recite the following incantation:
   a) "Pepper black, candle black,
      Banish debt so it won't come back."
3) Once the candle is dressed, light it and let the wax drip onto the card (or card replica) covering the entire card. As the black wax drips onto the card/paper recite the following incantation:
   a) "Clean my slate and eliminate
      The debt that I accumulate."
4) Once the card/paper is completely covered with wax, sprinkle more pepper on top of it and then close the tinfoil around it so that you can carry it around.
5) Let the candle burn until it is gone. Snuff it if you have to leave.
6) Bury the package and the candle remains at a crossroads, preferably far from home. Once you have buried them tap on the ground three times with your dominant hand and say "Paid. Balance owed:$0." And on the way home visualize yourself telling everyone in your life that your card is entirely paid off.

Sigil Magic

Like words, symbols can be extremely powerful as they represent an entire concept
and hold unique vibrations. This is one practice where the art of forgetting
really comes in handy!

Letter sigil

Purpose: to create a letter-based sigil to attract the desired financial outcome.

Moon phase: any phase will do, but first quarter and full moon are best.

Items needed:
Cauldron or pot
Pen and paper
Envelope

1) Determine your intention and write it out on a piece of paper in one sentence. This should be in present tense. Use affirmative statements such as "I am", "I have" and "I'm grateful for."
2) Rewrite the sentence removing all vowels.
3) Rewrite the sentence again removing all repeating letters.
4) Take a new sheet of paper and draw out your sigil by including each letter into one united shape.
5) You may beautify the final shape or leave it as it. Once it's done cut out the sigil.
6) Enter a meditative state while holding onto the sigil and visualize the desired outcome happening to you. Focus on the feeling of gratitude and increase the intensity of this feeling.
7) Once you've reached what feels like the peak of your gratitude, stare at the sigil and pour all of that gratitude energy into the sigil. Visualize the sigil glowing.
8) Immediately place the sigil in the envelope and stop thinking about what it looks like.
9) Using fire safety, burn the envelope until all of the paper is completely gone.
10) Bury the ashes in your front yard or somewhere close.
11) Forget about the Sigil completely. Refrain from thinking about it and block out the image from your conscious mind. Let the Magick do its work.

Automatic drawing sigil

Purpose: to use automatic drawing to create a sigil to attract the desired financial outcome.

Moon phase: any phase will do, but first quarter and full moon are best.

Items needed:
Pen and paper
Envelope

1) Determine your intention and write it out on a piece of paper in one or multiple sentences. These should be in present tense. Use affirmative statements such as "I am", "I have" and "I'm grateful for."
2) Enter a meditative state and focus on the feeling of having received the extra income you desire.
3) While in this meditative state, take a blank piece of paper and start drawing random lines all over the paper as you feel inspired to in the moment.
4) Once you feel like you've drawn enough, look at the paper and pick out a small section of it that stands out to you.
5) Recreate this section on a small piece of paper making adjustments if needed.
6) Hold the sigil in your hands with your eyes closed as you meditate on the feeling of gratitude for having received money.
7) When you feel like you have reached the height of your gratitude, open your eyes and push the energy into the sigil and visualize it glowing with energy.
8) Immediately place the sigil in an envelope and then either burn it or bury it.
9) Forget all about it and let the Magick do its work.

Fehu wealth rune

Purpose: to attract more wealth using the wealth rune on everyday items.

Moon phase: any phase will do, but first quarter and full moon are best.

Items needed:
Green ink, marker or paint
Everyday objects
Paper or canvass

1) Take a nice piece of paper or a canvass and draw/paint the rune in green.
2) Get into a meditative state and then use the index finger and middle finger of your dominant hand to trace the green rune (without touching it). As you are tracing it visualize it beginning to glow with green light energy. Continue to trace it multiple times and visualize yourself having lots of cash and money in the bank.
3) With your fingers, draw the rune on the surface of objects that you touch every day such as wallets, cell phones, door knobs, coffee mugs etc.
4) Use your dominant hand to "push" the rune deeper into the object, visualizing the energy of the rune blending with the object itself and charging it. Once these objects are charged, they will always provide a boost of wealth energy that will help you attract more financial abundance.

Petitions

Petition spells are extremely powerful and involve writing a statement of intent in a ritualistic setting to obtain the desired outcome. Once written, the petition is usually sealed and activated in some way. Saliva, blood or other bodily fluids containing dna are most commonly used. It can be addressed to the universe, to yourself, to a spiritual being or to no one.

Petition the Universe

Purpose: to write a petition to the universe to bring you more money. If you wish, you can specify the amount and time frame.

Moon phase: waxing moon or full moon.

Items needed:
Blank piece of paper
Green or gold pen
Scratch paper
Cookie sheet
Mint leafs
Basil leafs
Coffee
String

1) Fill the cookie sheet with coffee, add the leaves and let it sit for about 15 minutes.
2) Soak the blank sheet of paper in the mixture until it is stained brown, then let it air dry (or carefully dry it in the oven). If you want you can embellish the edges by burning or ripping them.
3) On a piece of scratch paper, write a draft of your petition. Try to incorporate important details about your desired outcome without making it too long. Use positive statements such as "Starting now, I will have/do/go…" and "I will experience xyz feelings".
4) On the blank piece of paper, write "Petition to the Universe" as the title.
5) Write out the body of your petition in the best handwriting you can manage. Make sure there is space left at the bottom.
6) At the bottom, draw a circle slightly bigger than a fingerprint. Below the circle write "So mote it be."
7) Read the petition out loud three times and then lick your thumb and press it inside the circle to leave a thumbprint made of saliva.
8) Roll up the paper and tie it with string. You can unravel it and read it out loud every night or as often as you like.

Petition your Higher Self

Purpose: to create a written contract with your Higher Self to activate your money magnetism and maximize your financial intuition.

Moon phase: any phase will do, but waxing and full moon are best.

Items needed:
Dried mint leaves
Lock of your hair
Cauldron or pot
Paper and pen
Lighter

1) Write out the following contract in your own words on a nice piece of paper.

Full Name (higher self)

I command the following changes with divine authority: I hereby activate my inner money magnetism. Money will be effortlessly drawn to me. I hereby maximize my financial intuition. I will instinctively know what to do to obtain more money in any circumstance. I hereby amplify my willpower. I will always have the energy and the motivation to get things done.

2) Read it out loud nine times.
3) Place your lock of hair and the mint leaves on the paper and roll/fold it up.
4) Using fire safety, burn it in the cauldron. While burning it, meditate on what it means to live by the statements in the petition.

Spiral petition

Purpose: to use the power of the spiral to draw more money to you. This petition isn't directed at anyone or anything in particular.

Moon phase: waxing moon or full moon.

Items needed:
Money drawing oil
Brown paper bag
Paper and pen

1) Draw a large circle on a blank space of the bag. Use your hands to carefully rip the circle out of the bag. Don't use scissors or any type of blade.
2) Write your name at the center of the circle.
3) Use a piece of scratch paper to brainstorm and summarize your intention for the petition. State that you are receiving more money and what you will do with it. Write everything in the present tense.
4) Once your petition is boiled down to 5 sentences or less, begin writing these sentences in small letters on the paper circle by starting on the outside edge moving inward. Repeat the sentences until the entire paper is filled up, and connect the last letter of the last word to your name.
5) Dip your thumb in a tiny bit of money drawing oil and stamp a thumbprint onto your name.
6) Hang it on the wall above your bed and visualize the desired outcome every time you look at it.

Jar petition

Purpose: to petition a god/angel of choice to assist you with acquiring more wealth.

Moon phase: first quarter or full moon.

Items needed:
Offerings for specific entity
Cinnamon sticks
Paper and pen
Mint leafs
Basil leafs
Incense
Jar

1) Research the deity that you will be petitioning to find out what offerings they prefer. Deities associated with water would work the best.
2) Fill a jar with water and insert the leafs and cinnamon sticks. Hold the jar and visualize your desired outcome. See the energy of this feeling transfer from you to the jar making it glow.
3) Write a draft of your petition on scratch paper. Include the desired outcome, the offerings being promised and thanks to the entity.
4) Write "Petition to *deity name*" as the title on your official petition paper, and write out your petition in the best handwriting you can manage. When you are done, roll it up and close it with string or tape.
5) Light the incense and run the petition through the smoke while reciting the following incantation:
   a) "Smoke rising from the sky,
   Carry my intentions high.
   I call upon *deity name*."
6) Put the petition in the jar making sure the entire paper is covered with water.
7) Keep the jar by a window where the sun will hit it.
8) Place offerings at the base of a tree as soon as possible.

Note: gold paper or ink work best. Ideally, your petition paper should be small enough to fit in a jar, but it's ok if you have to fold it.

Gods, Angels and Demons

When it comes to manifesting wealth, it can really help to have some divine assistance. Each god, angel or demon has a unique set of characteristics, abilities and preferences. Choose wisely.

Gods

Lakshmi

Purpose: to receive Lakshmi's assistance with becoming more abundant.

Moon phase: first quarter or full moon.

Description: Lakshmi, wife of Vishnu, is the Hindu goddess of wealth, prosperity and beauty. She is usually depicted as a beautiful woman with a golden complexion sitting or standing on a lotus with coins flowing from her hands. She usually has four arms, and elephants can be seen in the background as well as jewelry, food, coins and flowers.

Items needed:
Pink, gold or transparent vase
Gold jewelry (optional)
Sea shells
Flowers
Fruits
Coins
Basil

1) Take some time to research this deity online or at a library. Familiarize yourself with her attributes and get a feel for her personality and preferences. Try to make a connection.
2) Set up an altar for her:
    a) Fill the vase with drinking water (not faucet water).
    b) Tape or glue the image of the goddess to the vase.
    c) Put basil leaves, sea shells, fruits, jewelry and flowers all around the base of the vase.
3) Optionally, you can look up audio/video of a Lakshmi chant or invocation. Play it during your interactions with the goddess. You can also play it as you are falling asleep at night.

4) Sit in front of the vase and meditate on the feeling of abundance while holding her image in your mind. Give thanks for all of the money that has come into your life so far. Ask the goddess to help bring more abundance into your life. Declare that you are open to receiving all of the abundance that she sends your way.
5) Drop coins into the vase every day while repeating step 4.
6) When it's time to get rid of the offerings, leave them at the base of a tree.

Plutus

Purpose: to receive Plutus' assistance with attracting more abundance.

Moon phase: first quarter or full moon.

Description: Plutus (not to be confused with Pluto) is the greek god of wealth. He is blind, winged and almost always depicted carrying a cornucopia. Sometimes he is depicted as a baby sitting in the arms of the goddess.

Items needed:
Image of Plutus
Various fruits
Cornucopia
Pastry
Milk
Wine

1) Take some time to research this deity online or at a library. Familiarize yourself with his attributes and get a feel for his personality and preferences. Try to make a connection.
2) Fill the cornucopia with various fruits and pastries. Set milk, wine, and an image of Plutus beside it.
3) Find or write a prayer to this deity and include your request for financial assistance.
4) Recite this prayer in front of the cornucopia before bed every night.
5) When the fruit goes bad, leave it at the base of a tree and replace it with fresh fruit.

Mercury/Hermès

Purpose: to get quick financial results with some divine intervention.

Moon phase: first quarter or full moon (or on a Wednesday).

Description: Mercury is the Roman version of the Greek god Hermes. He is the god of financial gain, commerce, communication, travel and trickery. He is often depicted holding the caduceus in his left hand. This god is known for being a bit of a trickster so be sure to set clear boundaries when working with him.

Items needed:
Statue of Hermes
Paper and pen
Frankincense
Honey
Olives
Wine

1) Take time to research this deity and get familiar with his image and character.
2) Write down what you want to ask of him and what you're boundaries are.
3) Summarize your ideas into a prayer that begins with inviting him into your life. State that the offerings of olives, wine and honey are for him and then ask for his assistance. Add a brief statement about what your boundaries are. Conclude the prayer by thanking him for his help.
4) After setting up your sacred space, hold the statue of Hermes in your hands and bathe it in frankincense smoke while you read your prayer out loud.
5) Place the statue outside your door along with three bowls containing the offerings.
6) Replace these offerings as necessary for as long as you want to continue to work with this deity.

Note: If you're not in a position to put items outside your door due to neighbors or animals, you can put the arrangement on a windowsill or a shelf close to a window.

Wealth deities

There are gods and goddesses other than the ones listed in these spells above that are associated with wealth and abundance. It is up to you to determine which one is right for you. You can figure it out by researching all of them and determining which one stands out to you the most, or sometimes the deity will pick you and make its presence known unexpectedly. Look out for synchronicities and symbolisms. If a deity picks you, the relationship is likely to be a fruitful one. But just because they picked you doesn't mean that you have to work with them. If something feels off and you have doubts about working with an entity, trust your instincts.

The following is a list of some of the less commonly known wealth deities you might be interested in researching:

Ashiakle (African goddess)
Bhaga (Indian god)
Oshun (Yoruba spirit-goddess)
Bishamontenno (Japanese god)
Caishen (Chinese god)
Daikoku (Japanese god)
Aje (Yoruba goddess)
Dhisana (Hindu goddess)
Esme (Welsh goddess)
Anumati (Sanskrit goddess)
Hsuan T'ien (Chinese god)
Parendi (Hindu goddess)
Teutates (Celtic god)
Vales (Slavic god)
Tiamontennu (Mayan god)
Tsai Shen (Chinese god)

Angels

Angels can be of great help when you are trying to attract more abundance in your life and you resonate with angelic vibrations. Similarly to evoking a deity, it is best to do research on your chosen angel before you start praying to it. To receive assistance from an angel, all you need to do is ask. You can ask out loud or simply think it in your head. Use their name and ask them to help you. If you want, you can also look up prayers specific to the angel of choice. Keep in mind these are angels, they aren't particularly inclined towards accommodating greed. If you're going to ask for an angel's help, your request should be reasonable and it should benefit all parties involved.

Here's a list of angels that are known for being able to assist with drawing in abundance:

Archangel Ariel
Archangel Barakiel
Archangel Chamuel
Archangel Hamied
Archangel Gadiel
Archangel Gamaliel
Archangel Jeremial
Archangel Metatron
Archangel Michael
Archangel Pathiel
Archangel Raguel
Archangel Raziel
Archangel Sandalphon
Archangel Zacharael
Archangel Zadkiel

Angel meditation

In a comfortable, quiet space, assume a meditative position and begin to slow your breathing. Breathe in relaxation and breathe out any negative feelings.

With your eyes closed, see yourself walking up a staircase that leads into the clouds. You should feel yourself become lighter as you go up. When you're ready, see a golden door in front of you and know that this door leads to a heavenly room where you will meet your angel. Picture every detail of this door and see your hand grab the handle and open it.

When you walk in you see a beautiful room with several windows looking into a beautiful garden. Your angel turns around and greets you affectionately. At this point you can ask any questions that come to mind or you can ask for the assistance you need.

Thank the angel with all your heart before you leave, and when you're ready to go, open the same door that you came from and descend the staircase. Gently bring yourself back to the waking state and go about your day with gratitude in your heart.

Demons

I felt the need to include a section about demons for the sake of completeness. They can provide swift and powerful assistance but it always comes with a price. I'm not here to judge anybody's path, but to those who ask for my opinion, I say that, generally speaking, you should stick with the Light. Lesser demons, however, can be very insightful, provided you proceed with caution.

Summoning a demon often requires obtaining and/or wearing certain artifacts including bracelets and pendants with the demon's sigil. If you decide this is the path for you, you must first pick a specific demon and do thorough research to find out what the demon is all about and what its preferences are. Each demon prefers a different type of offering and may require a different set of tools for summoning.

A ritual usually involves wearing black robes, drawing an upside down pentacle on the ground and reciting verses from the Bible, the Ars Goetia, or other mystic books. Five black candles and incense associated with the demon are customary. The format to follow is usually similar to the ones used to evoke a deity. The demon may communicate with you via telepathy, physical signs or divination tools. Whatever you do, act and speak respectfully. Here's a rather short list of demons that are known for making wealth deals:

Buné

Clauneck

Mammon

Proceed with caution.

Notes

Made in United States
North Haven, CT
10 June 2025